My RV Travel Log

In Case *of* Emergency

My name is:———————————— **I am** ———————— **yrs. old**

Please Contact

My ———————————————— at this # ————————————

My ———————————————— at this # ————————————

My ———————————————— at this # ————————————

I have the following medical conditions

_____

_____

_____

_____

I have allergies   ### My prescriptions

_____   _____

_____   _____

_____   _____

                             _____

My Doctor is:
His # is:

In Case of Emergency

My name is:————————— **I am** ————— **yrs. old**

Please Contact

My ————————————— at this # —————————

My ————————————— at this # —————————

My ————————————— at this # —————————

I have the following medical conditions

_____

_____

_____

_____

I have allergies

_____

_____

_____

My prescriptions

_____

_____

_____

_____

My Doctor is:

His # is:

RV *departure* Checklist

## RV Interior		## Vehicle Interior
Items stored secured		Drinks, snacks filled
Cupboards closed		Travel mugs
Windows side, ceiling closed		Maps, routes, GPS programmed
Satellite dish down		Music, radio, books on cd
TV antenna down		Cell phone
Kitchen sink counters empty		Purse, wallet, ID
Frig items secured		Keys accounted for
Frig door secured		Sun glasses
Frig power off		Tissues, paper towels
Water pump off		Pets walked, secured
Slides in, clean roof first		Mirrors adjusted
Trash out		Clean windshield
Water heater/furnace/ac off		Check fuel level

Notes:

RV *departure* Checklist

RV Exterior

	Check fresh water tank, refill
	Drain black and gray tanks
	Disconnect sewer, water
	Shut off propane
	Retract awning, secure
	Retract TV/satellite antenna
	Secure bathroom vent
	Raise rear jacks
	Hookup trailer to vehicle
	Raise front jacks
	Remove wheel blocks
	Check tire pressure
	Check lights
	Secure RV steps
	Lock all exterior hatch doors

Vehicle Exterior

	Check brake safety switch
	Check hitch is secure
	Check for fluid leaks on ground
	Check power cable connection
	Inspect underside for loose parts
	Check all doors
	Check all fluid levels under hood

RV *mileage* Log

Date	Location	Odometer start	Odometer finish	MPG

RV *mileage* Log

Date	Location	Odometer start	Odometer finish	MPG

RV *mileage* Log

Date	Location	Odometer start	Odometer finish	MPG

RV *mileage* Log

Date	Location	Odometer start	Odometer finish	MPG

RV Park *review* Log

Campground: _____ **Date stayed:** _____

Location: _____

GPS: _____

Other notes: _____

RV Park Details

Site Details

Site # _____

Good sites:

Bad sites:

Nearby fuel:

Travel Time:

Notes:

RV *meal* Planner

SUN	MON	TUE	WED	THUR	FRI	SAT
breakfast	*breakfast*	*breakfast*	*breakfast*	*breakfast*	*breakfast*	*breakfast*
lunch	*lunch*	*lunch*	*lunch*	*lunch*	*lunch*	*lunch*
dinner	*dinner*	*dinner*	*dinner*	*dinner*	*dinner*	*dinner*
snacks	*snacks*	*snacks*	*snacks*	*snacks*	*snacks*	*snacks*

FOOD

Fridge	Freezer	Groceries	Beverages

Day 1

Date:

Weather:

My Mood today:

The best thing I did:

ALL THE THINGS I DID TODAY

Day 2

Date:

Weather:

My Mood today:

The best thing I did:

ALL THE THINGS I DID TODAY

Day 3

Date:

Weather:

My Mood today:

The best thing I did:

ALL THE THINGS I DID TODAY

Day 4

Date:

Weather:

My Mood today:

The best thing I did:

ALL THE THINGS I DID TODAY

Day 5

Date:

Weather:

My Mood today:

The best thing I did:

ALL THE THINGS I DID TODAY

Day 6

Date:

Weather:

My Mood today:

The best thing I did:

ALL THE THINGS I DID TODAY

Day 7

Date:

Weather:

My Mood today:

The best thing I did:

ALL THE THINGS I DID TODAY

RV Park *review* Log

Campground: Date stayed:

Location:

GPS:

Other notes:

RV Park Details

Site Details

Site #

Good sites:

Bad sites:

Nearby fuel:

Travel Time:

Notes:

RV *meal* Planner

SUN	MON	TUE	WED	THUR	FRI	SAT
breakfast	*breakfast*	*breakfast*	*breakfast*	*breakfast*	*breakfast*	*breakfast*
lunch	*lunch*	*lunch*	*lunch*	*lunch*	*lunch*	*lunch*
dinner	*dinner*	*dinner*	*dinner*	*dinner*	*dinner*	*dinner*
snacks	*snacks*	*snacks*	*snacks*	*snacks*	*snacks*	*snacks*

FOOD

Fridge	Freezer	Groceries	Beverages

Day 8

Date:

Weather:

My Mood today:

The best thing I did:

ALL THE THINGS I DID TODAY

Day 9

Date:

Weather:

My Mood today:

The best thing I did:

ALL THE THINGS I DID TODAY

Day | 10

Date:

Weather:

My Mood today:

The best thing I did:

ALL THE THINGS I DID TODAY

Day 11

Date:

Weather:

My Mood today:

The best thing I did:

ALL THE THINGS I DID TODAY

Day 12

Date:

Weather:

My Mood today:

The best thing I did:

ALL THE THINGS I DID TODAY

Day 13

Date:

Weather:

My Mood today:

The best thing I did:

ALL THE THINGS I DID TODAY

Day 14

Date:

Weather:

My Mood today:

The best thing I did:

ALL THE THINGS I DID TODAY

RV Park *review* Log

Campground: _____ Date stayed: _____

Location: _____

GPS: _____

Other notes: _____

RV Park Details

Site Details

Site # _____

Good sites:

Bad sites:

Nearby fuel:

Travel Time:

Notes:

RV *meal* Planner

SUN	MON	TUE	WED	THUR	FRI	SAT
breakfast	*breakfast*	*breakfast*	*breakfast*	*breakfast*	*breakfast*	*breakfast*
lunch	*lunch*	*lunch*	*lunch*	*lunch*	*lunch*	*lunch*
dinner	*dinner*	*dinner*	*dinner*	*dinner*	*dinner*	*dinner*
snacks	*snacks*	*snacks*	*snacks*	*snacks*	*snacks*	*snacks*

FOOD

Fridge	Freezer	Groceries	Beverages

Day 15

Date:

Weather:

My Mood today:

The best thing I did:

ALL THE THINGS I DID TODAY

Day 16

Date:

Weather:

My Mood today:

The best thing I did:

ALL THE THINGS I DID TODAY

Day 17

Date:

Weather:

My Mood today:

The best thing I did:

ALL THE THINGS I DID TODAY

Day 18

Date:

Weather:

My Mood today:

The best thing I did:

ALL THE THINGS I DID TODAY

Day 19

Date:

Weather:

My Mood today:

The best thing I did:

ALL THE THINGS I DID TODAY

Day 20

Date:

Weather:

My Mood today:

The best thing I did:

ALL THE THINGS I DID TODAY

Day 21

Date:

Weather:

My Mood today:

The best thing I did:

ALL THE THINGS I DID TODAY

RV Park *review* Log

Campground: _____ Date stayed: _____

Location: _____

GPS: _____

Other notes: _____
_____

RV Park Details

Site Details

Site # _____

Good sites:

Bad sites:

Nearby fuel:

Travel Time:

Notes:
_____
_____
_____

RV *meal* Planner

SUN	MON	TUE	WED	THUR	FRI	SAT
breakfast	*breakfast*	*breakfast*	*breakfast*	*breakfast*	*breakfast*	*breakfast*
lunch	*lunch*	*lunch*	*lunch*	*lunch*	*lunch*	*lunch*
dinner	*dinner*	*dinner*	*dinner*	*dinner*	*dinner*	*dinner*
snacks	*snacks*	*snacks*	*snacks*	*snacks*	*snacks*	*snacks*

FOOD

Fridge	Freezer	Groceries	Beverages

Day 22

Date:

Weather:

My Mood today:	The best thing I did:

ALL THE THINGS I DID TODAY

Day 23

Date:

Weather:

My Mood today:

The best thing I did:

ALL THE THINGS I DID TODAY

Day 24

Date:

Weather:

My Mood today:

The best thing I did:

ALL THE THINGS I DID TODAY

Day 25

Date:

Weather:

My Mood today:

The best thing I did:

ALL THE THINGS I DID TODAY

Day 26

Date:

Weather:

My Mood today:

The best thing I did:

ALL THE THINGS I DID TODAY

Day 27

Date:

Weather:

My Mood today:

The best thing I did:

ALL THE THINGS I DID TODAY

Day | 28

Date:

Weather:

My Mood today:

The best thing I did:

ALL THE THINGS I DID TODAY

RV Park *review* Log

Campground: _____ Date stayed: _____

Location: _____

GPS: _____

Other notes: _____

_____

RV Park Details

Site Details

Site # _____

Good sites:

Bad sites:

Nearby fuel:

Travel Time:

Notes:

RV *meal* Planner

SUN	MON	TUE	WED	THUR	FRI	SAT
breakfast	*breakfast*	*breakfast*	*breakfast*	*breakfast*	*breakfast*	*breakfast*
lunch	*lunch*	*lunch*	*lunch*	*lunch*	*lunch*	*lunch*
dinner	*dinner*	*dinner*	*dinner*	*dinner*	*dinner*	*dinner*
snacks	*snacks*	*snacks*	*snacks*	*snacks*	*snacks*	*snacks*

FOOD

Fridge	Freezer	Groceries	Beverages

Day 29

Date:

Weather:

My Mood today:

The best thing I did:

ALL THE THINGS I DID TODAY

Day 30

Date:

Weather:

My Mood today:

The best thing I did:

ALL THE THINGS I DID TODAY

Day 31

Date:

Weather:

My Mood today:

The best thing I did:

ALL THE THINGS I DID TODAY

RV Park *review* Log

Campground: Date stayed:

Location:

GPS:

Other notes:

RV Park Details

Site Details

Site #

Good sites:

Bad sites:

Nearby fuel:

Travel Time:

Notes:

RV *meal* Planner

SUN	MON	TUE	WED	THUR	FRI	SAT
breakfast	*breakfast*	*breakfast*	*breakfast*	*breakfast*	*breakfast*	*breakfast*
lunch	*lunch*	*lunch*	*lunch*	*lunch*	*lunch*	*lunch*
dinner	*dinner*	*dinner*	*dinner*	*dinner*	*dinner*	*dinner*
snacks	*snacks*	*snacks*	*snacks*	*snacks*	*snacks*	*snacks*

FOOD

Fridge	Freezer	Groceries	Beverages

Day 1

Date:

Weather:

My Mood today:

The best thing I did:

ALL THE THINGS I DID TODAY

Day 2

Date:

Weather:

My Mood today:

The best thing I did:

ALL THE THINGS I DID TODAY

Day 3

Date:

Weather:

My Mood today:

The best thing I did:

ALL THE THINGS I DID TODAY

Day | Date:

Weather:

| My Mood today: | The best thing I did: |

ALL THE THINGS I DID TODAY

Day 5

Date:

Weather:

My Mood today:

The best thing I did:

ALL THE THINGS I DID TODAY

Day 6

Date:

Weather:

My Mood today:

The best thing I did:

ALL THE THINGS I DID TODAY

Day 7

Date:

Weather:

My Mood today:

The best thing I did:

ALL THE THINGS I DID TODAY

RV Park *review* Log

Campground: Date stayed:

Location:

GPS:

Other notes:

RV Park Details

Site Details

Site #

Good sites:

Bad sites:

Nearby fuel:

Travel Time:

Notes:

RV *meal* Planner

SUN	MON	TUE	WED	THUR	FRI	SAT
breakfast	*breakfast*	*breakfast*	*breakfast*	*breakfast*	*breakfast*	*breakfast*
lunch	*lunch*	*lunch*	*lunch*	*lunch*	*lunch*	*lunch*
dinner	*dinner*	*dinner*	*dinner*	*dinner*	*dinner*	*dinner*
snacks	*snacks*	*snacks*	*snacks*	*snacks*	*snacks*	*snacks*

FOOD

Fridge	Freezer	Groceries	Beverages

Day 8

Date:

Weather:

My Mood today:

The best thing I did:

ALL THE THINGS I DID TODAY

Day [9]

Date:

Weather:

My Mood today:

The best thing I did:

ALL THE THINGS I DID TODAY

Day 10

Date:

Weather:

My Mood today:

The best thing I did:

ALL THE THINGS I DID TODAY

Day 11

Date:

Weather:

My Mood today:

The best thing I did:

ALL THE THINGS I DID TODAY

Day 12

Date:

Weather:

My Mood today:

The best thing I did:

ALL THE THINGS I DID TODAY

Day 13

Date:

Weather:

My Mood today:

The best thing I did:

ALL THE THINGS I DID TODAY

Day 14

Date:

Weather:

My Mood today:	The best thing I did:

ALL THE THINGS I DID TODAY

RV Park *review* Log

Campground: Date stayed:

Location:

GPS:

Other notes:

RV Park Details

Site Details

Site #

Good sites:

Bad sites:

Nearby fuel:

Travel Time:

Notes:

RV *meal* Planner

SUN	MON	TUE	WED	THUR	FRI	SAT
breakfast	*breakfast*	*breakfast*	*breakfast*	*breakfast*	*breakfast*	*breakfast*
lunch	*lunch*	*lunch*	*lunch*	*lunch*	*lunch*	*lunch*
dinner	*dinner*	*dinner*	*dinner*	*dinner*	*dinner*	*dinner*
snacks	*snacks*	*snacks*	*snacks*	*snacks*	*snacks*	*snacks*

FOOD

Fridge	Freezer	Groceries	Beverages

Day 15

Date:

Weather:

My Mood today:

The best thing I did:

ALL THE THINGS I DID TODAY

Day 16

Date:

Weather:

My Mood today:

The best thing I did:

ALL THE THINGS I DID TODAY

Day 17

Date:

Weather:

My Mood today:

The best thing I did:

ALL THE THINGS I DID TODAY

Day 18

Date:

Weather:

My Mood today:

The best thing I did:

ALL THE THINGS I DID TODAY

Day 19

Date:

Weather:

My Mood today:

The best thing I did:

ALL THE THINGS I DID TODAY

Day 20

Date:

Weather:

My Mood today:

The best thing I did:

ALL THE THINGS I DID TODAY

Day 21

Date:

Weather:

My Mood today:

The best thing I did:

ALL THE THINGS I DID TODAY

RV Park *review* Log

Campground: _____   Date stayed: _____

Location: _____

GPS: _____

Other notes: _____
_____

RV Park Details	Site Details
	Site # _____
	Good sites:
	Bad sites:

Nearby fuel:	Notes:
Travel Time:	

RV *meal* Planner

SUN	MON	TUE	WED	THUR	FRI	SAT
breakfast	*breakfast*	*breakfast*	*breakfast*	*breakfast*	*breakfast*	*breakfast*
lunch	*lunch*	*lunch*	*lunch*	*lunch*	*lunch*	*lunch*
dinner	*dinner*	*dinner*	*dinner*	*dinner*	*dinner*	*dinner*
snacks	*snacks*	*snacks*	*snacks*	*snacks*	*snacks*	*snacks*

FOOD

Fridge	Freezer	Groceries	Beverages

Day 22

Date:

Weather:

My Mood today:

The best thing I did:

ALL THE THINGS I DID TODAY

Day 23

Date:

Weather:

My Mood today:

The best thing I did:

ALL THE THINGS I DID TODAY

Day 24

Date:

Weather:

My Mood today:

The best thing I did:

ALL THE THINGS I DID TODAY

Day 25

Date:

Weather:

My Mood today:

The best thing I did:

ALL THE THINGS I DID TODAY

Day 26

Date:

Weather:

My Mood today:

The best thing I did:

ALL THE THINGS I DID TODAY

Day 27

27	Date:
	Weather:

My Mood today:	The best thing I did:

ALL THE THINGS I DID TODAY

Day 28

Date:

Weather:

My Mood today:

The best thing I did:

ALL THE THINGS I DID TODAY

RV Park *review* Log

Campground: _____   Date stayed: _____

Location: _____

GPS: _____

Other notes: _____

RV Park Details

Site Details

Site # _____

Good sites:

Bad sites:

Nearby fuel:

Travel Time:

Notes:

RV *meal* Planner

SUN	MON	TUE	WED	THUR	FRI	SAT
breakfast	*breakfast*	*breakfast*	*breakfast*	*breakfast*	*breakfast*	*breakfast*
lunch	*lunch*	*lunch*	*lunch*	*lunch*	*lunch*	*lunch*
dinner	*dinner*	*dinner*	*dinner*	*dinner*	*dinner*	*dinner*
snacks	*snacks*	*snacks*	*snacks*	*snacks*	*snacks*	*snacks*

FOOD

Fridge	Freezer	Groceries	Beverages

Day 29

Date:

Weather:

My Mood today:

The best thing I did:

ALL THE THINGS I DID TODAY

Day 30

Date:

Weather:

My Mood today:

The best thing I did:

ALL THE THINGS I DID TODAY

Day 31

Date:

Weather:

My Mood today:

The best thing I did:

ALL THE THINGS I DID TODAY

RV Park *review* Log

Campground:

Date stayed:

Location:

GPS:

Other notes:

RV Park Details

Site Details

Site # _____

Good sites:

Bad sites:

Nearby fuel:

Travel Time:

Notes:

RV *meal* Planner

SUN	MON	TUE	WED	THUR	FRI	SAT
breakfast	*breakfast*	*breakfast*	*breakfast*	*breakfast*	*breakfast*	*breakfast*
lunch	*lunch*	*lunch*	*lunch*	*lunch*	*lunch*	*lunch*
dinner	*dinner*	*dinner*	*dinner*	*dinner*	*dinner*	*dinner*
snacks	*snacks*	*snacks*	*snacks*	*snacks*	*snacks*	*snacks*

FOOD

Fridge	Freezer	Groceries	Beverages

Day 1

Date:

Weather:

My Mood today:

The best thing I did:

ALL THE THINGS I DID TODAY

Day 2

Date:

Weather:

My Mood today:

The best thing I did:

ALL THE THINGS I DID TODAY

Day 3

Date:

Weather:

My Mood today:

The best thing I did:

ALL THE THINGS I DID TODAY

Day 4

Date:

Weather:

My Mood today:

The best thing I did:

ALL THE THINGS I DID TODAY

Day 5

Date:

Weather:

My Mood today:

The best thing I did:

ALL THE THINGS I DID TODAY

Day 6

Date:

Weather:

My Mood today:

The best thing I did:

ALL THE THINGS I DID TODAY

Day 7

Date:

Weather:

My Mood today:

The best thing I did:

ALL THE THINGS I DID TODAY

RV Park *review* Log

Campground: Date stayed:

Location:

GPS:

Other notes:

RV Park Details	Site Details
	Site # _____
	Good sites:
	Bad sites:

Nearby fuel:	Notes:
Travel Time:	

RV *meal* Planner

SUN	MON	TUE	WED	THUR	FRI	SAT
breakfast	*breakfast*	*breakfast*	*breakfast*	*breakfast*	*breakfast*	*breakfast*
lunch	*lunch*	*lunch*	*lunch*	*lunch*	*lunch*	*lunch*
dinner	*dinner*	*dinner*	*dinner*	*dinner*	*dinner*	*dinner*
snacks	*snacks*	*snacks*	*snacks*	*snacks*	*snacks*	*snacks*

FOOD

Fridge	Freezer	Groceries	Beverages

Day 8

Date:

Weather:

My Mood today:

The best thing I did:

ALL THE THINGS I DID TODAY

Day 9

Date:

Weather:

My Mood today:	The best thing I did:

ALL THE THINGS I DID TODAY

Day | 10

Date:

Weather:

My Mood today:

The best thing I did:

ALL THE THINGS I DID TODAY

Day 11

Date:

Weather:

My Mood today:	The best thing I did:

ALL THE THINGS I DID TODAY

Day 12

Date:

Weather:

My Mood today:

The best thing I did:

ALL THE THINGS I DID TODAY

Day | 13

Date:

Weather:

My Mood today:

The best thing I did:

ALL THE THINGS I DID TODAY

Day 14

Date:

Weather:

My Mood today:

The best thing I did:

ALL THE THINGS I DID TODAY

RV Park *review* Log

Campground: Date stayed:

Location: _____

GPS: _____

Other notes: _____

_____

RV Park Details

Site Details

Site # _____

Good sites:

Bad sites:

Nearby fuel:

Travel Time:

Notes:

RV *meal* Planner

SUN	MON	TUE	WED	THUR	FRI	SAT
breakfast	*breakfast*	*breakfast*	*breakfast*	*breakfast*	*breakfast*	*breakfast*
lunch	*lunch*	*lunch*	*lunch*	*lunch*	*lunch*	*lunch*
dinner	*dinner*	*dinner*	*dinner*	*dinner*	*dinner*	*dinner*
snacks	*snacks*	*snacks*	*snacks*	*snacks*	*snacks*	*snacks*

FOOD

Fridge	Freezer	Groceries	Beverages

Day 15

Date:

Weather:

My Mood today:

The best thing I did:

ALL THE THINGS I DID TODAY

Day 16

Date:

Weather:

My Mood today:

The best thing I did:

ALL THE THINGS I DID TODAY

Day

17

Date:

Weather:

My Mood today:

The best thing I did:

ALL THE THINGS I DID TODAY

Day 18

Date:

Weather:

My Mood today:

The best thing I did:

ALL THE THINGS I DID TODAY

Day | 19

Date:

Weather:

My Mood today:

The best thing I did:

ALL THE THINGS I DID TODAY

Day | 20

Date:

Weather:

My Mood today:

The best thing I did:

ALL THE THINGS I DID TODAY

Day | 21

Date:

Weather:

My Mood today:

The best thing I did:

ALL THE THINGS I DID TODAY

RV Park *review* Log

Campground: _____ Date stayed: _____

Location: _____

GPS: _____

Other notes: _____

RV Park Details

Site Details

Site # _____

Good sites:

Bad sites:

Nearby fuel:

Travel Time:

Notes:

RV *meal* Planner

SUN	MON	TUE	WED	THUR	FRI	SAT
breakfast	*breakfast*	*breakfast*	*breakfast*	*breakfast*	*breakfast*	*breakfast*
lunch	*lunch*	*lunch*	*lunch*	*lunch*	*lunch*	*lunch*
dinner	*dinner*	*dinner*	*dinner*	*dinner*	*dinner*	*dinner*
snacks	*snacks*	*snacks*	*snacks*	*snacks*	*snacks*	*snacks*

FOOD

Fridge	Freezer	Groceries	Beverages

Day 22

Date:

Weather:

My Mood today:

The best thing I did:

ALL THE THINGS I DID TODAY

Day 23

Date:

Weather:

My Mood today:

The best thing I did:

ALL THE THINGS I DID TODAY

Day 24

Date:

Weather:

My Mood today:

The best thing I did:

ALL THE THINGS I DID TODAY

Day 25

Date:	
Weather:	

My Mood today:

The best thing I did:

ALL THE THINGS I DID TODAY

Day 26

Date:

Weather:

My Mood today:

The best thing I did:

ALL THE THINGS I DID TODAY

Day 27

Date:

Weather:

My Mood today:

The best thing I did:

ALL THE THINGS I DID TODAY

Day 28

Date:

Weather:

My Mood today:

The best thing I did:

ALL THE THINGS I DID TODAY

RV Park *review* Log

Campground: Date stayed:

Location:

GPS:

Other notes:

RV Park Details

Site Details

Site #

Good sites:

Bad sites:

Nearby fuel:

Travel Time:

Notes:

RV *meal* Planner

SUN	MON	TUE	WED	THUR	FRI	SAT
breakfast	breakfast	breakfast	breakfast	breakfast	breakfast	breakfast
lunch	lunch	lunch	lunch	lunch	lunch	lunch
dinner	dinner	dinner	dinner	dinner	dinner	dinner
snacks	snacks	snacks	snacks	snacks	snacks	snacks

FOOD

Fridge	Freezer	Groceries	Beverages

Day | 29

Date:

Weather:

My Mood today:

The best thing I did:

ALL THE THINGS I DID TODAY

Day 30

Date:

Weather:

My Mood today:

The best thing I did:

ALL THE THINGS I DID TODAY

Day 31

Date:

Weather:

My Mood today:

The best thing I did:

ALL THE THINGS I DID TODAY

Ready for a new Logbook. You can order one
from plannersandjournalsforeveryone.com
Order yours today!

Made in the USA
Monee, IL
14 March 2022